D0839202

FIRST PONY OUT

SAMUEL STENGER RENKEN

WSC PRESS - *Wayne, NE*

First Pony Out
Copyright © 2020 by Samuel Stenger Renken
All Rights Reserved

ISBN: 978-1-7320275-4-1
Published by WSC Press

Layout and cover design by Sharon Cole
Cover artwork "Coyote" by Michael Goettee
Foreword by Ben Gotschall

No part of this book may be used or reproduced in any manner whatsoever
without written permission except in the case of brief quotations embodied
in critical articles and reviews.

WSC Press
1111 Main Street
Wayne, NE 68787

wscpress@wsc.edu
wscpress.com

TABLE OF CONTENTS

EXPRESSING THE PONY: A FOREWORD TO MY FRIEND SAM RENKEN'S SECOND COLLECTION OF POEMS

BY BEN GOTSCHALL

I'M ASHAMED TO ADMIT that I didn't really know much about the Pony Express before I read this book, and I still don't. I'm willing to bet Sam Renken didn't know much more about it either, in the academic, historical sense, than I do now, before he wrote these poems. But write them he did, and we are much the beneficiaries of this fine volume of Western verse. As someone who grew up in Nebraska, as Sam did also, the Pony Express to me was kind of a footnote in history, not as glamorous and complicated as the Civil War, the Indian Wars, or the cowboys and outlaws in Western movies. Yet, its legacy still remains, visible in towns such as St. Joseph, Missouri, Gothenburg, Nebraska, Laramie, Wyoming, and beyond.

To say the Pony Express had long odds of success is an understatement. The whole affair lasted only a year and a half and was immediately ousted by the telegraph: wood and wire replacing humans on horseback, a fitting metaphor for the American West (and for cowboy culture in particular). The Express lost its investors hundreds of thousands of dollars and cost dozens of its employees their lives. In all, the 35,000 pieces of mail actually delivered lost an average of about $5.70 each, or about $165 at today's rate of inflation.

In many ways, the Pony Express was an impossible enterprise—a logistical nightmare doomed to failure by weather, physical distance and geographic obstacles, to say nothing of the sociopolitical chaos created by Manifest Destiny, the California Gold Rush, and the Anglo-centric concept of "settling" an "uncivilized" frontier by displacing its indigenous inhabitants, who were themselves viewed as obstacles—the problematic colonial mind-set alluded to in this book's epigraph "To the Pioneers." To write a book navigating such themes, a book of poetry, no less, a significant part of which is personal narrative, is also no small undertaking.

There is something to be said about lived experience, and the way it comes alive in these pages. In "Can't Hear a Stone," the poem which introduces the recurring theme of the poet taking disabled and delinquent juveniles on immersive-experience trail rides through the Wyoming wilderness, when the poet tells us, "Shock collars aren't allowed, / even for deaf wards of the state / in Wyoming, western as it hopes to be," we can't help but believe the words, not because we want to, but because through them, we have had the experience now, too, and we can't look away as he describes using a toy pistol to shoot a stream of water "in an ear/canal at almost ten yards, quiet as a rock." We can't un-see an image such as a herd of buffalo, as it "pours through / sand blowouts like a swarm / of galloping gnats," and we can't un-hear the rhythm of lines like, "here's to the prayer, / not of darkness / but to the beet red moon / big as a battleship at bay / and the pre-dawn confident." The poems in *First Pony Out* are such that establish their own certain credibility; even though several of them are found, and others imagined, these poems come together to create a world, the inhabitants of which slip easily between past and present, from stark realism to the fantastic, among places and events including a campfire somewhere in the Nevada desert, the assassination of John F. Kennedy, outrunning bloodthirsty wolves on the Kansas Plains, and burying a chicken named Lady Gaga in the backyard.

The theme of horses, like anything written or pictured of the Pony Express, pervades these pages with a ubiquity that can suddenly give way to an acute, almost visceral awareness when we as readers transition from passive observer to present participant. Horseback riding, whether for work or pleasure, requires a certain level of trust, and, inversely, trustworthiness, which isn't to say faultlessness or perfection, but more to be open about weakness and to be willing to confront the how to overcome it. Sam Renken's poetry, like a trustworthy horse, requires something of the reader. It requires of us a presence, with lines like the ones in the final stanza of the book's title poem: "Sylph, you will be whipped / wet with white froth / and quivering in your flanks / by the time we hit Kickapoo." Just as a horseback rider is not merely passive, a reader of Sam's poems doesn't merely pass through—or by—lines like the ones in "Camouflaged Hunters" in which the poet describes hoisting a bloody field-dressed deer carcass onto his horse's back, "where I / bind him to the living / hooves, to the time / before his wet birth, / from the spot of his last / air between the frosty / earth and setting sky." I, for one, can't help but place myself, in that moment, into the first person of the poem's narrative voice.

There is a certain amount of accountability here. We can't ignore that our ancestors were accomplices to shaping the world that came to be after the Pony Express connected New York to California, joining the humming industrial and political centers of the East and the wild and reckless booming West, brokering with it the most ancient and invaluable commodity: information. We know deep down what was gained and what was lost when the sod turned and rails bridged rivers. These poems remind us, in both cerebral and visceral language, that we are still connected to the old wounds of the first furrows, to the death and destruction of wild things, of first people, of bare horizons that both defined and defied possibility. We are the beneficiaries of what came before, and after, that possibility was framed inside the borders of a nation not above dividing itself.

Too much of today's poetry is absent of accountability, ungrounded, devoid of the heft of life, weightless with ideas and abstractions floating away save for maybe a string of an image to tether it to something real. In comparison, the poems in *First Pony Out* are hay bales—70-pound blocks of stored solar energy and seed—and the poet is in the loft, tossing each one to the barn floor with a thud. I invite you to cut the twine and feed them out.

FIRST PONY OUT

TO THE PIONEERS

…and now the barren plains that reeked with death;
and western hills that only hostiles knew
are made to show the vibrant, living breath
of homes and happiness and dreams come true…

the cry of savage nature now is stilled…

96 RANCHES

They say no mochilo
made by Israel Landis survives,
perhaps because no one can prove
the one in the old station on the main ranch,
the ones we lit by cell phone and lighter,
was used by a Pony Express rider. The door to the station
was unlocked, the floor re-poured into smooth cement,
but the structure is where it was 150 years ago
when Frenchmen dragged logs, the marks
from their de-barkers dug the rough angles
says Larry Gill, the ranch owner, who heard it from his dad
and takes a swivel chair, glad to quit his shop cleaning
because he just had his knee rebuilt a few weeks back
and it'll be a long day tomorrow.

Two red Freightliners, one 52-foot semi-trailer,
two horse trailers (one gooseneck, one bumper pull)
a John Deere 4020 and 4440, empty fuel barrels on four legs,
rows of t-post, re-bar, and coiled wire. Lots more, shadowed.

Our west, conquered with two-minute
rest stops between stations, was dark then
save the moon and its vanishing act across
the wind-blown plains of the Platte and Sweetwater
when wiry young men pretending to be fearless
risked their voice in the running
of knowledge, they would neither know nor
could ever read. The land was young and thin and tough
as a nail. After visiting the Pony Express station and
watching its station manager fade in my mirrors,

I stopped at the McDonalds in town per the suggestion
of the ranch owner's daughter, Claudine. I saw
the riders, hell-bent toward the future,
running onto brief, trodden ground, later a ranch now near leaving.
Inside, the walls name riders beside their picture and quarter-pounders.
In the men's room is the oath:

I, Jack Keetley, *do hereby swear, before the great*
and living God, that during my engagement,
and while I, John Phillip Koerner,
am an employee of Russell, Majors and Waddell,
I, Michael Whalen, *will, under no*
circumstances, use profane language,
that I, Billy Fisher, *will drink*
no intoxicating liquors,
that I, Buffalo Bill Cody, *will*
not quarrel or fight with
Broncho Charlie Miller
or Johnny Fry,
or with any other employee of the firm,
and that in every respect
I, Bill Campbell, *will conduct myself honestly,*
be faithful to my duties,
and so direct all my acts
as to win the confidence
of my employers, so help me God.

CAN'T HEAR A STONE

I used to keep small stones
in the front pockets of my chaps
for when the trail ahead was slick
rock or littered with low-hanging branches.

Unable to sign most of what I wanted
to say, I would aim for torso and finger spell
potential and unseen dangers ahead,
but the first time I hit a deaf gal in her upper
lip, I knew my method had a hitch in its get-along.

Shock collars aren't allowed,
even for deaf wards of the state
in Wyoming, western as it hopes to be,
so I bought a hand-held nine millimeter
replica that shoots water from a hunter's
orange tip and could put a round in an ear
canal at almost ten yards; quiet as a rock.

ALL OF SIZE

When the children grow all of size,
damn near everything gets easier.

Not only can they clutch bucket
and bridle, but also hammer
and rifle. Little fingers
deadly as cold
on quick triggers
in the rock-raised pit,
half dozen strides
from the cabin.

The butter is churned.
The pig skinned.
Wood split.
Water drawn.

Fire arrows
have been flying
all evening so they don't sleep
and we pray over hot water and
bread with fresh butter,
imagine the lit arrows to be
only lightning bugs, but
by now the little ones are good
at drawing out the fat.

THE CAT, THE OWL AND A TRAIN

On a second story porch,
discussion turned from young
marriage and old values
to the fear of China
and our country's loss
of its super-power status.

Phyllis the cat walked the rail
without fear of falling on the groomed grass
below, without care for the night
and its hollow whistle through the self
same houses of the suburb.

Wanting my father to know
his generation created ours,
deemed worthless by so many, I
hoped he could see the path of a nation
and its uncontrollable spiral told the end
of its reign. He refused to relent, denied the inevitable
fall. Atop the lights dimmed above the soccer fields across the tracks
nearby, an owl stocked the low cut grass for movement,
for rodent scent and blade shuffle.

The owl waited for his meal that would not be handed to him,
a train whistle sounded at the crossing
before the fields and the owl dropped
into something soft and palatable,
too small to be seen in the half dark before the tracks shook.

At home two days later,
the city delivered matching trash cans

bearing the Steamboat bucking horse
logo in white on brown
to all within its limits,
and instructions were given
as to when to have it on the curb,
what to fill it with,
and how it should be bagged.

BUFFALO

Moving a herd
sometimes is easier
said than done, but it can
be done.
      That said,
moving bison is something
altogether different than punching cattle
through an open three-strand gate
of barbed wire.
               Just as likely to jump
               the fence on either side
               of the opened gate, closed
by the limits of isolation,
the herd pours through
sand blowouts like a swarm
of galloping gnats
and the wooliest stop
in the six-mile valley,
waiting before the open
land and beginning to think
about turning.
               Even a one-eyed whore could see
               the buffalo hides, long as dogs,
               and the trampled seedless
               dust making opaque
               the dark bottles
               signature as desolation,
               covering the rail split heard.

CHAINING UP

The old-timers drug
their feet across the ice-
covered lot toward tractors
idling like shuttering beasts
after a cold shot from a rifle.
They carried hot coffee in travel
mugs as big as their hairy faces,
and whole bags of pretzels
to negate the two pounds
of chocolate. In a Wyoming
mustache, they nodded
to me like I was friend
not foe when I asked
if the hot young team
chaining they're 18 wheels
in the snow knew enough
to know they wouldn't be
leaving until the snow let
up tomorrow afternoon
when they wouldn't need
chains. With a new baby
in the house, I like
to play big to folks
like I've been up half
the night with crying
and she's always wanting
to eat, but I don't now,
and hope I never will,
have mammary glands.
She leaves me

to sleep for hours
on end, and I am learning
to be content in my own home
skin. The leaky faucet
no longer drips and the seat
on the toilet is fresh oak,
lacquered somehow to keep
the piss around the edges
from rotting it to the quick.

They say that some things
cannot be taught and
the young bucks didn't ask
how long I-80
would be stuck in this icy wind.
I am looking for candy-
corn to make beaks
for moon pie owls
on a stick, a product
of my mother-in-law
and oldest daughter,
who is 24 fortnights
over 2 years old.

The truth is happy
all around me.
I thought an annex
might be nice
for the cardboard
house not big enough
for me to turn around in,
but it turns out these close

quarters feel nice on my
shoulders, keep me by
the treads just
like I never thought
I wanted to be.

BURNING BUFFALO CHIPS

When there was nothing
to burn but digested bunch
grass and wild rye,
the smoke would rise,
white and thick
as the steam from the pole
of the horses loping in.
Their mane, a thin bead
of fog fingering off,
dripped sweat from its tips.

The smell was no different
than burning dusty tumbleweeds
or the dried pods of yucca.
And the gathering was easy
because they grazed the high
plains
from the badlands well past
the land of flat water,
and all of them shit loose
cakes baked dry in the sun.

BUSINESSES VIEWED FROM ATOP THE WAGNER BUILDING AT SUNSET WITH A PBR IN SEPTEMBER 2012

Qdoba, Bootbarn,
Travelodge: DSL,
Daylight Donuts,
Majestic Lube,
Antiques: Junction
Tobacco, Mizu Sushi,
Alibi: unseen,
Bank West, Plains
Tire, Altitude, Home
Bakery, Music Box,
Cross Country
Connection, Mountain
Valley Bridal, Herb
House, Hallmark:
The Curiosity Shoppe,
Big Hoss Mountain
Sport, Nails Tech,
Gallery West and The Cowboy.

CHANGING HORSES, PUMPKINSEED STATION, NEBRASKA

A greybeard station manager
totes news of Lincoln's election maybe
from the rein-dropped horse hanging
a long neck toward the foreground
of the painting. The correspondence
of half a dozen businesses travel
at 5 bucks a sheet in the mochilo pockets.

A calf-skinned left hand thick
in her mane, right hand grasping
a dangling whip that all but touches
the ground, the rider is one leg from horseback
with the near knee-high boot, spurred,
already in the stirrup of a Santa Fe style,
A-framed saddle girthed to the next mare.

Her front hooves are kicked up and out
toward the station assistant, his hands
on either side of the bit. Her ears are up,
like the thatched grass of the roof
which whistles enough in the wind
to make her dance,
to keep her in standing tremble,
unwrapped and just off the hitching post.

CONTENTS OF A CRUSHED ICE PACK IN WATER GLASS

When I am looking
down at myself,
that small spot
between the end
and the beginning
of time, my eyes
bloodshot at the tiny
idea of nothing's
embrace, I am not
humbled enough
to believe this small
cause implausible,
so I write.

To the point now
where I forget
the sound of the pen,
my fingers click desks
and look for a keyboard
in their sleep.

I cannot complete
the pie for you
anymore,
and there are kids
poisoning each other
in the room next door.

AS EVER

for Maggie

It's only air most
days, and windows

look below the strong
arms of the American Elms
for your smile to pull in air
between us
and deep breaths,
this faithful settling foundation.

Our skin is cheap velvet
to the words, long breath
of my cornfield dreams;

alive, blue bathed in orange
against that ancient trunk
lit by impossible light
from the leaning porch.
Your eyes meet mine again.

CROSS AS THUNDER

Half the hands quit
when the arrows flew,
but others gifted booze
and food enough to fill
the ribs of growing
warriors. And they were
after the lighting,
a long ways off
of the end of the breath
they feared losing, rumbling
before the stage coaches
and steam locomotives
to follow. There's a lot of talk
of scalping and picked bones
dropped white and clean
into shallow graves
mounded over with rock,
but history forgets
the ones hunting meat,
not flesh to count coup
the ones willing
to chase down a rider
when the mail drops
through a slit in the mochilo
and starts to blow away
in the wake of the rider
wishing only to escape
what some call fate.

DEAR STUDENTS,

Now that it is Friday,
I want you to know
something about desire,
my wish for you to be
here even after the mornings
when the wrens ride the flat
fat backs of wintering horses
because it can be, sometimes,
too windy to fly and staying
above can be so much work.

Know we are all built to fall,
supposed to wreck, from urges,
these water-colored dreams
encouraging us to hitch
along until a better ride
pulls beside, opens
a door.

The sun will
still be shining some
place when the moon's
man comes around
or we could never
see him, and there
is a lost twinkle
in every galaxy
to remind me
of you.

Sincerely,

DEATH CROTCH

Even the worst riders have to let go
like the best, allow their horse enough
reins for them to place each delicate hoof
where they see they must to keep atop
the side-cut-switch-backs and off the loose
rock and boulders below the trail.

Before I knew his bottle-bottomed glasses
were broken and he was given a nickname
to fit his "hard enough" lean that shifted
any saddle, even cinched enough to take a breath,
left on any horse far enough to make his butt
on ribs and his right boot above his head,

I almost watched him kill a gelding
in an accident that very well would have
killed him too. This was the day of birth
for Roger Dodger Danger, when he locked
his ape arms and held his horse's mouth
until it gaped and the horse stumbled
to free itself nearing the crevice's edge.

He dismounted when I shouted,
and the gelding headed down
more quickly than any equine would
unless they'd been nearly pulled
over the crumbling rock brink.

EDIE

You are in there.
I've seen
your foot pushing
against the soft
wall of your mother's
stomach in protest
and when you come,

I will shave my beard,
smooth my face
against the velvet
spot between your ears
and mouth to melt
right into the vinyl
recliner in that hospital
room. It will be

the kind of day
when I can drive
down the street
ten miles under
with open windows
and a cigar, breath
like the fresh, filthy
king of an unchallenged
land, and think

about the short, damp
canal between us,
about the miles
born before us.

FAT PUPPY STEW WITH SPOTTED TAIL

Beneath the sky of the great Brule
Chief; Mitchell, Logan, and Williams
(later to be the names of towns
and prairie counties) dined,
dipped into the great rich brew
of culture 40 miles from the fort.

The same low dales given
to homesteaders digging trenches
supported with adz-squared logs
around the rough hew corners
of their barn built by broad ax

were his. Above the narrows,
in a buffalo wallow, and
behind the biggest sage;
palms clutched.

In the waiting night
outside the feasting teepee,
everything hung like a cloud
around the river, and then the village
vanished when the moon was setting.

Mitchell, bound to war,
boasted of good Indians
being dead, of how it is essential,
of course, to kill all nits,
if you want to destroy lice,

and finally Spotted Tail was poison
himself, an agent of America and
then the Sioux, assassinated
by Crow Dog's bullet.

FINDING PATH

No stations or managers to guide,
I follow global positioning satellites
to no avail. It is the forest service troughs
that give the edge, and humbly we trudge
down the softest path into the valley
along the same trails antelope and elk,
deer and moose, sheep and cattle have
to get down from the rocky heights.

Half a day's ride from camp, a Californian quits
by refusing to ride any further, and I oblige by
taking his borrowed horse and helmet and boots
and calling the Albany County Sherriff with coordinates
to escort him down from Pole Mountain. Unseen
by him, I track him with my mare's ears
until the cruiser, rutting its way across the washboards,
meets him in a clearing between two boulders
balanced precariously on either side of the drop.

Like any kid, deviant and defiant or not, he wants
his horse and boots, will even put his helmet back on
to keep riding the trail with us, but his screaming tears
aren't enough to make me forget what I don't know
how I know, that growth is a trail that winds and stalks,
switches back and stops where it must to make it.

Cutting down the path to the rest of the group,
I can see the barn between them and the sun
dropping behind the shadow of the impossible
purple mountains, and I know it to be more
than dumb luck that found us here, six miles

from home on the worn track of invisible game
where the white rock split into beach-fine sand
deeper and more arduous than home's long, dry valley.

FIRST PONY OUT

"Hardly will the cloud of dust which envelops the rider die away before
the puff of steam will be seen upon the horizon."

—M. Jeff Thompson, St Joseph's mayor

Sylph, you are all ears,
certain the hoopla's for you
when the mayor and Majors
talk about the length of the ox-bow,
the necessity for a central route.
Butterfield held messages
an easy fortnight every pass
until the southern stations
were raided and burned
by natives willing to dismount
and finish anything with a knife.

On the eve of the first ride,
the amassed crowd plucked
hair from your California pony
tail until you threatened to kick
the next yanking arm slap off.
The crowd plucked still,
for luck to the parcel,
20 pounds of tissue-thin paper
wrapped in oily silk
to keep the notes clear
of bleeding ink
when the mail swims
across rivers and their tributaries
all the long way to the waiting
western settlers on the short side

of the mighty Rocky Mountains.
in the lingering ripple of the Sierras.

The notes are already
at a steady gallop
toward us, news
of western gold
and waiting fortune.

Sylph, you will be whipped,
wet with white froth
and quivering in your flanks
by the time we hit Kickapoo.

FIRST S'MORE

Every pack trip, there's at least one
who's never had one, and they all ask
how many they can have. This summer,
I follow my wife's lead and tell them
they can eat as many as they want,
however, many they think they can
without blowing sweet chunks
into the smoldering fire.

This is the most natural
of natural consequences,
which is what we are supposed
to teach them through these trips
where experiential therapy is
what they make of it.

Not knowing how the fire-roasted
marshmallows melt with the Hershey's
around the graham crackers to create
a soft but un-dissolvable gut rock, their
sticky lips grin raw, innocent sweetness.

The horses don't even stomp flies
at this point around the campfire,
chewing only the few spare stalks
remaining in their hay bags
and dropping loose apples
in squat from the dirty stream
water they drank too much of
and lush greenery they devoured

along the trail between camp
and home in the hands
of their youthful riders.

If one has spilled their sweet guts
along the half-lit edges of camp,
I've yet to witness it, but I do not know
that when we turn back to the sun
almost everything breathing in camp
can't help but let out
a soft moan when they sigh.

FLIPPING COWS

Those still
living
circled the bare
spot in the snow
where the trailer
had been,
lined the barbed wire
dividing the ditch
and the foot-hilled
pasture.

The tractor was gone
too, tracks from where
a wrecker drug it
from the brown slush
streaked with oil.

Clumps of black
snow marked
its towed path
toward Woods
Landing,
and cloven hooves
of a dozen
stuck from drifts
liked buried arms
from snowmen.

JACKIE-OH

Everything must have
gotten brighter that day
when you swore in
his replacement
after you held him,
his shattered skull
bits, while the motorcade
grabbed another gear
in the day's lost
charm. At night
when the branches
break from the trunk
of reality and you are
left beautiful, alone
with dreams, nightmares
of forgetting what memory
holds for so many
in our country's collective
sign,
I imagine you
in a restless
comforter, wearing
dark glasses
on white down
pillows,
looking out
toward the blackness
like sleep.

FOUND POEM: SMALL MOUND

His head and under jaw was found
entire with the most of the teeth.

Dug some 5 feet
and found a great many bones,
and in one of the joints of his spine

was a spear
which had punctured
to the spinal marrow.

GOODBYES

Don't be fooled by the goodbyers,
faithless for the next time
eyes meet eyes,
like old denim handshakes
and nothing is as everything was,
but everything's the same;
just the same.

Here in the star city, I
can feel you sleeping
between the stoplights
and potholes, breathing above
this soft spot of crust.
You and these gnarled roots
dig into so much more than dirt.

So here's to the prayer,
not of darkness
but to the beet red moon
big as a battleship at bay
and the pre-dawn confident.

Let there be always more
to say in the next hello,
the unseen handshake
(stove warm cream)
made more sweet
by the gut drop felt
when the goods are
gone, not for good,
but for now.

"…HIGH AND EFFICIENT SERVANT OF THE OVERLAND, AN OUTLAW
AMONG OUTLAWS AND YET THEIR RELENTLESS SCOURAGE, SLADE WAS
AT ONCE THE MOST BLOODY, THE MOST DANGEROUS, AND THE MOST
VALUABLE CITIZEN THAT INHABITED THE SAVAGE VASTNESS…"

—Mark Twain, *Roughing It*

Jules Beni founded the trading post
that came to be Julesburg and ruled it
before you, Captain Joseph Slade,
were sworn in to replace him.

Beni broke bad at the news
and dropped you with a shotgun
and left you for dead. Bleeding there you lay.
When you did not die, it was Jules
you went for and bound to the bucking post
of a prairie corral where you shot at his joints
and then used your bowie knife
to remove his ears for souvenir.

You, the later terror out there, ruthless,
a deft blind hammer, the kind of out-surviving justice
where the strong eat the straggling weak.
Forced into retirement,
imbibing redeye in the wilds
near Virginia City, you rode
the best horse you could steal
into bars, shot out all the lights,
dropped down dried up cartilage dark as dirt,
ears kept from the founder and demand,
with those stiffened remains,
another bottle for your horse.

When they finally hung you,
your wife, Virginia Dale, rode your old horse like a flea-bitten dog.

She, guns blazing, wouldn't allow it,
though you were still hanging there,
wouldn't hear of you being buried,
at least in this devil rich country.
You may be sealed yet
in a tin coffin filled with the best
whiskey she could afford, for you to winter with her
before she took you by wagon to Salt Lake
for burial, when the thaw came around again.

CAMOUFLAGED HUNTERS

They drop me out-
side the pivot trail north
of the fingerling canyons
on their way to walk fields
mowed in long, wide lines
between the clumped red
grass tall as a man's hip,
hoping to shoot roosters
before lunch.

Before heading home
for Thanksgiving, a non-
fiction student called to ask
me if I knew how to skin.
Since I did, she wondered,
would I on an antelope
she shot?

The only buck
I ever killed
was with the same
.243 I carried into the rain-
cut edge of farmland
for turkeys. I saw him,
his rack even and smooth,
from my buried hold
crunching down the orange
leaves on the other side
of a deep cut. I thought,
*Oh, Buck! If you work
your way down*

to the clearing,
I will take you with
one shot for jerky
and sausage.

I've been belly-
crawling the dawn
away, many mornings
before now, tracking
of the cackle of a gaggle
of toms and hens grazing
the edges of the Earth
where the gathered water
kept the trees alive
and growing.

Wrapped in a torn blue
tarp, when she opened
the back hatch to her early
90s electric pink Ford
Escort wagon, too small
to be much more than a few
meals, the pronghorn was stiff
as my expression. My brow
wrinkled realizing respect,
for now, meant stripping
its hollow, wintering hair.

The buck walked right
down where he needed to
for me to get a clean shot

and use a steady, slow
finger to drop him. Rearing
after the thud, he fell
on the spot.

The one I want,
with the jiggling gobbler
about as loose and long
as his neck and the same
red as my shirt, stuck
his head up three times
without shifting. I hollow
him from eye to eye above
his flopped neck
while he looks over
the horizon now
shifting from orange
to yellow.

Piercing leg skin,
I bound him with clothesline
through the space split
between tendon and bone
and hung him from a hook
on the rafters.
Not gutted,
I started the first cut, split
his anus and lifted him
from the hang-
hold to pour his cold
organs like old frozen

leftovers into a 55-gallon
drum lined with a black
plastic bag. The red
drawstring was too red
for the blood
that was
left.

I propped him,
rack up the canyon
in the long shadows,
split him and let him
drain down the slope
toward a trickle of ice-
edged water from a spring
not 40 paces through
the bur oaks and sumac
where he had lived.
My horse, hobbled and
chewing pasture, bent brome
brown and dry atop the spot,
knew not what I was doing
in the land below carved
by eons of dripping water
and centuries of spring
melting snow.

On my knees,
I cleaned the mess
of his neck with my knife
and hot plucked his feathers

in the webs of my fingers
like the tangled mane
of a horse, loved
for its length. Fluffed
when I finished, the crust
of Earth, a small tuft
of sage, wore the tom's
coat like a crown.

She takes notes
on a folded brochure
from the Wyoming
Territorial Prison
with the nub of a blue
pencil while I peel
down from his haunches,
having hung him again
above the small burnt
sienna puddle on the smooth
concrete floor. My nails dig
between muscle, sinew and skin
and pull the hide off, only
needing my knife to keep
it coming, clean and whole,
around the four bullet holes
from the bullet's entrance
and exit.

While all the fluid left
him, I shouldered the rifle
and hiked toward my buckskin,

slipped the rawhide knot
from its linking loop
around his black fetlock
above his butter cream body
and pushed the half-hitched
rein free from the rubber-
wrapped saddle horn.
Switching back two steps
behind me, Buckwheat
walked with enough wait
the weight of his front
hooves never even tapped
my boot heel, and beneath him
damp knotted twigs bent
without breaking above
the dark rotting flanges
that fell
from the naked arms
bent off the crooked
trunks weaving their way
toward the spent gift
of a healthy carcass
harvested.

His lean body–chiseled
from foraging and stuffed
with crumbs and raisins
absorbing oil form pork
sausage and juice from Granny
Smith's cubed–filled the biggest
baking pan in Grandma's kitchen

where the family offered
thanks before his body
was carved whole
and lead-free.

The hide is bagged
with the innards and head
severed by bone saw
with a deer antler handle.
I take no cut, carrying instead
the weight of its stripped existence
back to the unnatural blue
tarp lining the hatchback. Sky made
more cerulean by the bronze falling
from the Thornless Honeylocust
between the street and the root-
cracked sidewalk. I stand there
until she putts away and wash
my hands of it from the faucet
below the Canada Red
Chokecherry.

Buckwheat snorts
white steam in nostril
shots between whiffs
when we get right
by the bled-out buck,
knowing without words
death's throaty stench. My
breath quickens with my heart,
using an old calf rope over

a low hanging branch
and leverage to hoist
the dead across
the tacky leather
of my saddle, where I
bind him to the living
hooves, to the time
before his wet birth,
from the spot of his last
air between the frosty
earth and setting sky.

HIGH PLAINS ANIMAL HUSBANDRY

Never give away rattlesnakes,
instead gather them in a buried
oaken bucket and build a pit lid

to keep a misstep out of the fangs
and venom. The shade will do them
good in the summer, but they'll still

want that sun, so dig it deep
with vertical walls, spade smooth.

HOW THE MULE

Sat when he wanted
to run, ran when he needed
to sit, and slept like he knew
he needed to be at work.

Slept sitting on the edge
of the bed, on the chair
in the living room,
never half drunk.

On his feet always,
he refused to bear only
his weight, wanting the heft.
Content in carrying the load,
a long way off happiness
but a good ways from anger too;

he is never sessile in function,
but settled as the night's
dew on broad waterside leaves.

How he double-checked
the locks, slapping himself
like a beast in the cold
wind and be-moaning the size
of the half-pound bag of M&M's
after driving all night and eating
them over the same routes
as ancestors and animals
before them.

Away in innocent chairs, he
swatted when the flies were biting,
but kept his weighted head
down and waited.

HOW THE ROWDY BOYS DOWNSTAIRS BLED

The night was fair,
colorfully serene,
for those of us upstairs.
We danced under
ceilings we couldn't
jump to touch and lounged
on retro furniture and a couch
that wrapped itself around
its arms like a velour shell.

We spray-painted the bathroom
and covered all the lamps
in tapestries, so the walls
shook with the texture
of tiny elephants
and gold horns.

I felt like a tuba,
passed out at three
with a piece of egg
sandwich on my shoulder,

and I woke
to the drum of foundation,
felt the walls beneath me
quaking like a broken yoke.

Three of us slithered
out the double back doors
and down the steps cemented

onto the west side of the house.
We stepped into the basement
apartment like we were on ice
skates in October, and the music
was so loud we couldn't make out
what it was. We crouched from squished
ceiling, and the pound of a bass
drum against a thousand gallon
stock tank tinged. We walked the hall

toward the concussion,
opened the door and saw
a keg like a hacky sack
hitting the already bloodied
head of one of the rowdy meat
jobs, while the others punched
and yelled, despite their faces.

They asked my roommate
for more, looked at us
like they loved it,
and took torso shots
from a projectile
empty beer keg
for adrenaline.

The sun was rising
and the shag,
darkened with blood and
speckled with sea foam

chunks of plaster,
crawled the walls,
worked its way
out the half windows
and into the soft,
white damp grass
of Nebraska March.

HOW THE BALLERINA BROKE HER ARM

I closed the door on my own self,
left him between the cracked
leather of my old boots
and the unmarked
crates full of random
past collectibles
from the years between
when I found myself
in need of revision
and now.

Before the wind shifted
toward fall, a ballerina
stretched her long legs
over the squat chestnut
back of a gelding,
freeze-branded
by the Bureau
of Land Management.

With only a halter,
the lead rope
in her left hand
on the left side
of his fatty, flopping
neck. Sometimes I let
my old self out
from the closet
to do all the stupid
shit he wants, to forget

the dangers worth
remembering.

She began to trot,
beautifully bouncing,
and her flip-flopped toes
pointed toward the browning
ground, now accelerating,
while I caught from my eye's
corner, the fall.

I, WILLIAM CAMPBELL,
AM THE ONLY ONE LEFT TO TELL THE STORY

Long after the others were gone,
the Western Union Telegraph Company
was still asking me questions
about (as they called them) the glamorous days
of the Pony Express,
all 545 of them.

At 6 feet tall,
I was too large
until December 1860,
when the other riders ground down
and petered out
in the blowing snow and wind.

11 miles east of Fort Kearney at Valley Station,
a hundred miles along the Platte to Box Elder,
three miles west of Fort McPherson.
My eyelids clumped in the corners,
freezing like the ice-pack in the hollow
of the horse shoes. I kept my hands
holding those reins, the leather
stiff as brain-dried hide.

Carried Lincoln's first message to Congress,
the ground hard, hooves echoing
in a jarring gallop. That night, a pack of buffalo
wolves feasted
on an indistinguishable carcass. They took chase.
My horn helped a little. The horse shied. At the smell
of blood and the thirst of it, nothing to do

but flank and out-run them.
Ragged Jim took his head and the bit
until the pack fell off and we could see
the flick of light at the next station.

I poisoned a carcass.
Twelve dead wolves about it
when I made there again,
so I left the fur with Sioux squaws
who used sinew and stitched
the bunch into fine robes.

IT BLOWS

The wind in Wyoming
keeps everyone honest
and close to home,
so if you find yourself
becoming more full
of shit where the mild
weather makes you stink,
join us here in February.

The snow used to be
in fluffy feet above
the dirt and dead plants,
but it has sucked
down now into white
ice, smooth and tan.

Grimy paths of it
lead across the backyard,
beneath the weight of this
melting and freezing,
my gutters smile
at me following
my own trail
to the trash can
out back.

The sky, so wide
and blue crystal,
moves the clouds
past us in the night.

The sky, high
as a Clydesdale,
lopes through
wind turbines
whining in circles.

I leave the bagged junk
there, of course,
for those who gather
what's left, the crows
and raccoon and fox
first, then the men
who bring their brown
truck to follow the long
road north of here
where they will bury
it and everything
it ever was to me.

KIDNEY BELT

A number nine,
the Broncho buster's
tight leather girdle
to keep the guts
where they should be,
wrapped right to the point
where a full breath squeezes
and only the rawhide laced
between the two pieces can give.

And it won't give much,
but it won't take much more
either, even if you suck in to tie it
tighter and hold on until the hell-
bitch is gritting her teeth, jumping
like a jack rabbit under pistol fire
and snorting the fenceless
land with a full head of steam,
her wild bruising juice.
Nothing hurts at all
until you let that belt loose.

MARGIN NOTES I FOUND IN KLOEFKORN'S POETRY BOOK, "NOT SUCH A BAD PLACE TO BE," BOUGHT FOR A BUCK ON AMAZON

Not all of the poems
have notes in their margins
because she was not required
to discuss them in class.

I say "she" because of the little curl
on the "p's" leg and the way
the "f" and "j" loop just so
tenderly toward the ends

of the words in blue pen,
"Life is a Joke." She has
correctly labeled a few
of the similes and caught

one of every four metaphors
walking the pages in her rubber
gloves. She writes reminders
like, "crotchety woman, allusion

and reality, grim humor, and
tone abrasive," but she missed
the life of your book. Perhaps
she didn't mean to ignore

the puffing utter of the cow
chewing pasture dew down
through its stomachs to answer
the questions without notes.

Perhaps she didn't mean
to create meaning stale
as beer vapor but forgot
the heartbeat we all have,

even in our poems, forgot
how people connect to places,
a barn full of shadows, the fast-
winged faith of sparrows at dusk.

MR. ELLSWORTH, FORMALLY OF SCOTT'S BLUFF

Dressed in silks,
these half-breeds,
looking more beautiful than a shirt
around a stovepipe,
rode into my station
one pouring night.

They killed an antelope
that very morning in the drizzle.
The wood was scarce around the station,
but we burned it over buffalo chips
then ate it.

Next day, I got wind of two deserters
stripped and stocked and given 50 lashes
by an Irishman I knew, who was used to the business
end of a black snake whip tipped
with five small braided buckskin crackers.

Poor bastards. Not wishing to enlist anymore,
I waited for the sound of hooves, for the horn.
All hands through are thunder cross
from the mud and clouds stacked
with rain all morning, but before night came again
the sun shined, drying road and grass good
and green from the standing water settling.

All seemed fine then. It came back through
that horses stolen near Fort Bridger were returned.
A wood headstone marks the spot in Echo Canyon.
Cornered, he wouldn't give himself up
to be hung by the train, so they shot him.

MILLION-ACRE BEDROOM

After I'd ridden through it
in the tired nights—when the moon
even was afraid to show its face—
I knew this at least: The stars,
though many, don't have any
power without me lying down here,
face-up in the hardly-ever dark,
looking back.

        The east is as quiet as crickets
        out here, but the towns
        and cities wear halos
        of light above them now
        where we brought the stars
        to just above ground level
        in case we drop a quarter
        walking from bar to car.

MULE

He has never known not having
a job, until now. Market lumbering
like sunk wagon wheels in need

of doping in the deep sand, riverside,
he returned 40 dollars to the Pizza Hut
in Broken Bow, the clerk over-charging
above the Pony route on the Platte.

Honest as a two-buck bill,
a 15 percent tipper,
because what it's worth
is worth nothing
more; he is right there,
but I don't see him yet.

After unloading the wagon,
he unhitched the team,
tapped the thick peg
into his foreboding palm,
and pulled the wheels
to soak in the swirls
of a gully in the shallows
of the South Platte.
There they will suck
some of the river's weight
into July dry drawn up pores
until the solid-wrapped iron tire
and the wobbling spokes
are snug together again.

NEVER MAKE A LIST OF POSSIBLE POEMS

Turkey Hunting
The Day Jerome Broke
Killing a Love Fichus

Frankenpine
Grady's Garage
The Night and the Pain Flipped

A Stick of Butter in the Bathroom
Van Pelt at McDonalds
Dog and Brad at LRA

Jackie-O
Innuendoes

THE NIGHT BEFORE

Halloween was wet cold from 14 inches of snow that was freezing in drifts
beneath the big clear sky exhaling winter's frigid breath
down into the valley and escorting all the clouds over the Snowy Range
to the west. The sun was setting when he finally passed, but it was early
in the morning when I found him penned in by a drift taller than his back
and the northernmost corner of barbed wire on the property
where the horses ate away ten months of icicle belly cold.

Unwilling to put any weight on his left front leg,
I knew something essential was broken in there,
so I dug a path with the Bobcat and backed the trailer in
as close as I could to load him. He got in too, stood
the ten miles to the vet and hardly struggled
when the school-fresh vet thumbed the vein in his neck
and filled him with half the juice of euthanasia needed
to stop his heart and hurt. Struggling with her gloves
and the second syringe, she missed the vein and filled
a subcutaneous pool with the rest of the blue
liquid needed to end the job. He fell against the trailer
wall, not dead but heart slowed enough to make him weak
before she could draw another syringe, and by the time
she returned, the pulse of his blood would hardly circulate
enough to pass the shot though his being,
half alive. He passed his bowels, pissed without dropping,
and began two hours of breathing the staccato breaths
that keep a body warm enough to let you know it's going.

When she came out with a four-inch needle and told me
she'd try to hit his heart, I knew she'd either slept through
horse anatomy or was plagued with the irrational thought
patterns that accompany failed death administered

through the shaky hands of imperfect beginners. I told her
to hold the shot and wait with us in the cold steel cave of the horse
trailer for him to quit. We didn't speak, looked at his spastic chest
and temperature dip before it was over.

His legs stiffened overnight inside the stock trailer beneath a blue tarp,
and they cracked like snow-heavy limbs, the kind that didn't shed leaves in time,
when I hooked a chain to his fetlocks and drug him out from the nose
onto the carcass pile at Laramie's dump where they covered him
with just enough dirt to hide him from the folks bringing in
their old tube-style televisions, broken limbs and empty cans of paint.

PALLID.

Progression a marvel,
I watch the latter world
and know I'm not of it anymore.

Two minutes to change horses at Dobytown
could never be fast enough. Eighty orphans
with two stout horses each would be dogged
after a week straight of riding to beat the pulse
of the telegraph wires cutting Ruby Valley

and Deep Creek. I gulp hot coffee
at Fairmont, mercury around zero, and the horse
I rode in on steams, standing there.
No on has to hold him.

ODE TO LADY GAGA

In the coup enclosing the empty woodshed
north of our carless garage,
she was done flopping and being pecked by those
still living behind the chicken
wire and sample wood from the last remaining furniture
factory in America. Fresh eggs
and an understanding for life and its cycles our goal,
our three year old was feeding them.
When it happened we were in the house unpacking
from a wedding. Gaga took a shot
to the neck from a pink cowboy boot, dying quicker than we
wanted with the name we'd given her.
Zuri screamed for us to fix her chicken, not yet
understanding that we could
not. We buried her beside the black locust tree
and beneath a bison
skull in our flower bed. Digging with a princess
shovel, my daughter using
a Dora one, I got down three feet and called it good.
My wife cried at the loss
of innocence with our nine month old in her arms,
and I was spitting mad
that I had left her to feed on her own. After seeing the flop,
she kept saying sorry for stepping
on it but went right back to her project with mud
pies after the service

When I asked her what she wanted
for dinner the next day, she said, "Dig up Lady Gaga; she could probably
be chicken nuggets by now,"
and I knew she knew what some never do, life can be over in one step
and sometimes we are better for it.

LONDON 1880: BRONCO CHARLIE MILLER

You're not on the historical list
of the Long Riders' Guild
because you found pride
in riding two British horses
to death in a race
against a bicycle.

You don't give a lick.
Pole Star wasn't your mount then,
who never balked a stretch between
the west of San Francisco
and the crowding eastern bridges
of New York City. Horses quit

often before the end, and
had the English mounted you
properly, no thing would have died.

PRECAMBRIAN GRANITE

Laramide orogeny, a rising up
100 million years ago or more,
brought to the surface these blocky
rocks, angular and sharp, balanced
on their precious, precarious edges
as if to fall with the slightest nudge.

In a partnership where even
the undeserving are catered to
with love, time brings season
to everything. Life, unearthed
in dancing embrace, is a constant
secret dream only visible in the small
places where we stop the world
to really see each other.

Among this stone-hold, you held
stone, climbed hand-in-hand
like you will again,
a day's travel from home.

Together against the night,
the sun rising and setting in turn,
may you weep and find laughter,
scatter to gather again and again,
and mend each other when you're torn,
no more or less than two hearts
in eternity, uprooting to plant.

Stone held for your embrace,
lip to intimate lip, and foundation

found you beneath blue sky
as impossibly deep as the distance
between two floating souls
and the rock-solid ground.

OF BEING

Prior to the convocation,
my class, little moved by
"Sould Meets Body" by Death-
cab for Cutie, fidgeted
in disgruntled sighs
at the new assignment
to create a story of past
self with present self's
benefit of knowledge.

Hindsight's 20/20.

Reluctant to admit
revelation or disclose
hidden understanding
of life as change, my
students claim to have
learned nothing
from experience
to this point.

Projected on the portable
screen in the dim gym,
"I Over-Dosed and
Survived," is below
a photo of a young girl
with crystal eyes gazing
toward the crowd
as confidently blue-
green as the Caribbean
water. Her hair is

curled, lipstick thick
as rose petals
above white teeth
smiling with a gap
between the front two.
In the flesh the girl,
biting a white terry cloth,
stiffens in her chair. Folding
cramped fingers like a dinosaur,
her arms break over, useless.
The small padded wheelchair
holding her, locked at the wheels
by her mother, seems
impossibly small, her frame
so frail and disappearing
from immobility.

Unable to talk
other than rough
finger-spelling, she
raises her middle
finger when asked about
her boyfriend, the one
who crushed a 200-milligram
pill of morphine for them
to snort. She quit breathing
long enough to stop
almost everything
but her soul, her mind
spinning still
behind so much wreckage

and havoc. The PowerPoint,
in another's voice, gave color
images of her beside friends
and family, before and after.

Her grandfather's flat smile
holding her in a wicker chair
in front of her 18th birthday cake,
gives weight to his eyes, wet
with loss and the physical
reminder of her future
lost to the unthinkable.

To be (before these students
half-heartedly committed
to recovery) so honestly
broken, cuts me
and makes me light
in the head like I've mashed
each of my fingernails
into ripe mulberries
in a door jam.

I am unbending
when we return
to the classroom
and a student claims
to have not listened,
bruised by indifference,
unable to believe anymore
she is less nothing
than something.

PONY BOB HASLAM

No bullwhacker,
Londoner buried in Chicago,
your route from Friday's on Lake Tahoe
to Buckland's Station near Fort Churchill
had alkali-clad hills hidden with savages
and their dead, 75 miles inland of the Pacific.

Upon 90 bloating Eastern corpses,
massacred men and women and their curled progeny,
you rode. Their souls would not quit
the dispatch to the next station.

Alone, save for the horse
and 30 seconds switch time
and the wash-eyed attendants,
you rode to stop it all and start it.

OLD PISS PANTS

She does it without realizing and told why
one day, reliving the day she doesn't remember
when her father's bat knocked something loose
in her three-year-old mind. She jokes about it,
has grown to do so and dismounts when it happens.

It was weeks later that I cried, my own blonde
three year old touching my damp face
with her little fingers soft as dream
you know but cannot tell anyone.

Maybe this senseless weight was
the abuse still alive. Perhaps the salty
taste was the confirmed relay
of visualizing skull softening
beneath confused inertia.

Nervous at first to believe in anything,
let alone herself, we hoisted her
with dampening shoulders behind
the thick withers of a black gelding,
so kind his eyes looked beyond
the horizon and into the layers
of time before this pain
we all knew now to be
present. The group jells

along the long trail,
and in the third day's sun
after two drizzling days,
two of her peers, now partners,

laugh in telling her where I can overhear
that they just peed in the saddle
the last few days because skin is so
wet it doesn't really matter anyway.

We didn't stop. I hoped my sunglasses
hid my tears, and one of them said
she did it more than once
because the brief warmth
was easy to crave.

RICHARD M. MAY: FOUND POEM

Early this morning
one of the company
and myself repaired
to a newly thrown up
mound with spade.

Dug 3½ feet and
found an Indian
buried there.

He has his implements
of war and taking game
in his arms, laying on his right
side with his head to the north.

PURPLE RAINBOW

I agreed to the name change
because the kid who was riding her listens to Pink Floyd
and that pony had a dark side.

When her right hind shoe came loose,
I spent the better part of the evening
working with her to get the thing nailed
back on for the next day's parade.

When she kept kicking me,
I gave her enough Ace to droop the eyes of a horse,
but she kept fighting, jumping and kicking, reaching
around to bite my hat, so I gave her another half dose.

It wasn't until she was Scotch-hobbled
that the shit really hit her.
Though her eyelids did sag,
I was just glad to get a nail through
and not worried about her condition
until she toppled over, one leg tied
up with cotton rope to the same rope
wrapped around her belly, and rolled
down the patchy grass and flowering pink
cactus ravine into the shallow flowing mud
of the creek below.

Still, breathing deep
the surge of unconsciousness
trickling past her spotted frame
I propped her head on the bank,
told the kids who'd run over to see

the wreck that, yes, I thought she was alive,
sat on her upturned gut and began, upside-down,
to hammer home the five remaining nails between my lips
through the steel dimples and into the limp hoof,
praying to all things holy that if and when she woke
from the spill, I'd have the shoe on tight enough
to keep her from kicking it loose or sucking it off
when she scrambled onto her legs again
in the knee-deep mud of the bottom
to get back up to the desperate place
where we began our struggle
between the dry ground and her hoof
split below the dirty old nail holes.

RIDING AT NIGHT WITH NEWTON MYRICK

Rolling along my right,
the great Nebraska
in silent sublimity
chums toward the Missouri,
toward the Mississippi.

It rained all day
and fell in torrents
toward evening
on the already luxuriant
growth of buffalo grass,
grazed short and thick
by the Red Man's cattle.

A dozen years ago out here,
all a sense of hearing
would convey to the mind
was the whip-crack,
the clanking of chains, and shriek
of disagreeable wagons.

Now in these lowlands
rich as the Blue River bottoms
and level as a bowling green,
hooves are all that's heard,
hooves and leather squawking
against leather and bagged post
rustling all 75 miles, all six hours.

ODE TO JOY

In the dark
we bundled up
in my garage,
put on coveralls
and down coats,
brought gloves
and toboggans
to keep our fingers
and ears out of the wind
and blowing snow.

We weren't drunk
to the bone, though
I drove with both hands
and chewed a stick-hard
piece of frozen Juicy Fruit.

It was Sheepdip,
scotch on the rocks
with lime twists that had us
done with the project's
planning before we left
the Calvarymen south
of town, and we all
agreed that tonight,
as much as any other,

was the perfect night
to remove a set
of decade-old mud flaps
and re-install them

on a late '80s,
maybe early '90s,
Bronco before the driver
was any wiser.

She casually mentioned
her desire for Wyoming
bucking horse flaps,
and the three of us
knew they couldn't be
new, needed to come
from a truck at least
as old as her Arizona
four-by-four. We rolled

in the snow beneath
a blue and silver one-
ton Chevy, used
adjustable crescents
and a cordless drill,
let the bolts fall
into a small drift
along the west
side of a Quonset,
leaving several
to that white pile.
We removed the angle
iron that held the flaps
against bumper's buttocks
and loaded the frozen
two-eyes stick atop the folded

backseat. We cackled
to the snow filling
our tracks, mud
atop carpet, gum
in the hair of a dog,
and relished in victory
with another beer
and a homemade frozen
fruit cup after midnight.

They hung,
two flat hard black
nuts riding the muddy back,
like panties after a mud slide,
and the truck somehow looked more
commando with their addition.

In the sun the next day,
they dangled with wet
frozen drips off their rubber
tongues and in the hand-typed
note I found in my mailbox
she said simply, "I am
so happy!" on paper yellowed
and brittle on the sun-cracked
edges from the windowsill
of its marginal life before this.

SAMUEL STOPS AT A ROAD RANCHE

Off a Concord stagecoach,
he regained his stance,
adjusting from the dancing
spring leafs in the cross
of the prairie's packed path,
away from civilization
and headed into it.

Five bays
and a similar chestnut
stay hitched, take turns
dipping their loose
lips into well water,
drawn into rope-handled buckets
from a hand pump
as red as the out-stretched
tongue-tips of the horses
when they finish the offering.

And they each do finish
a bucket and would another
if the folks roughing it
west didn't want to stop
tonight at the bluff
of Hyram Scott.

Samuel watches
the clock in his pocket
while one of the brothers
managing the stop works

the pump's arm
and the other holds
a bucket's wet rope
beside the silver ribbon.

STUCK ALL NIGHT

Two days ago I found a crow,
flapping like a torn black
garbage sack, with its head
stuck between two slats
of the back corral's wind-
break. Little blood drops
spotted the boards
on either side, and it sat
still as a hypnotized chicken
when I walked up behind it.
I thought it was dead,
but it was warm
and twitched at my fingers
when I pulled it up
and out opposite of how
it came to be down and in
like that. Atop the fence, its head
bobbed, heavy as a monkey's,
and it fell forward
until it's wings caught
in a gentle arc
to the dirt where it
stayed and flattened
to the earth. I never saw
it fly again, but it nodded
its head and walked toward
the tall brush filling space
beneath the bottom board
of the rotting livestock
chute.

SATURDAY EVENING POST, JUNE 3, 1922

Hog tight, calfskin boots in the sun after a walk across the Niobrara River.

Bull strong, bull-wacker's backs after the long walk to the other side.

Horse high, grasses, even wind-bent, brushing belly and tickling flank.

Pioneers, O, how even
your words sound
bigger than those
who follow them.

THE LINE

After 20 miles we shouldn't make them
stand all night, but we do because in three days
we will be at the Frontier Days parade to follow
Hell's Half Acre's flat down the cowboy-lined
streets of downtown, paved now, where once
a year women still dress like working girls
and men with painted on dirt dress
like cowboys and rustlers and pour beer
over one another from rippling thick glass mugs.

People are dancing, to native drums and new songs
about men and whiskey and women and livestock.
The hitching posts are blocked by Harleys
and flatbed four-wheel drive pickups
with large chrome bull testicles hanging
below the receiver hitch. One man stands
atop his Palomino to crack a bullwhip
and spin a novelty six-shooter around
his right forefinger. The horses

don't move a muscle all night,
let the bloodsuckers bite
and the bats sonar
their squeaky dive into midnight
dinner while they cock hip to rest.

Pre-dawn, I peel back the bivy sac
to see by the blood moonlight
four hooves beside my head
and angus on the skirts of camp.

Rose, my parade-hating mare,
is on her belly beside me
with her muzzle resting
on the soft brome spread
from the bale I broke open
to sleep on, and her lead rope
snakes its way under her barrel,
a visible line unknotted. Invisible
is the hitch between us, both
waiting for the soft allure of home
for the safe breath of what's to be
understood as sacred only in its absence.

SOME STATIONS WEST OF FORT LARAMIE

Wagon Hound, Labonta, and Box Elder,
Natural Bridge on LaPrele Creek,
Deer Creek, Big and Little Muddy,
Platte Bridge and Poison Spider, before
Willow Springs, Horse Creek, and Independence
Rock, Devil's Gate and Split Rock,
Three Crossings and Long's Creek,
Meier's Crossing, Rocky Point,
St. Mary's, Burnt Ranch.

WHERE THE FIRST BLOOD SPILLED

Walking home from the wedding
with a fresh cocktail from the Eagle's
Club, we are picked up by a deputy
and invited into his Expedition
for a lift to the hotel. He all
but commends us for not driving,
drunk as we were, but won't wail
the sirens when he lets us off
under the lobby's pull-in.

This is not the place for revelry,
not the time to celebrate
escaped demise.

When he opens the backdoor
for me to get out, my thoughts
are barred to the local jail
where an old friend is
probably sleeping
fitfully to pass the 30 days
he must to find his freedom
again after one too many behind
the wheel one too many times.

We don't feel the tug of age,
aren't old, but it's coming for us.

He's divorced now. I look toward the young
officer watching my own wife and imagine
the nights my friend's wife left alone when he was

too drunk to reason and too weakened to kill.
Remembering the sound of his fist
breaking agsinst the palm
of his older brother,
metacarpal cracking

the fire in a hidden place
between
them and the thick air of the hug
they held before his hand was cast
after his father grounded the butt,
placed his chin atop the wide mouth
and pushed the 20-gauge trigger.

I know how the bars are straight
as the rows of head-high corn.

TO THE CHOICE MEMORY OF FINCELIUS GREY BURNETT: 1844-1934

Pioneer, historian, gentlemen,
friend who knew the language,
the haunts of the Red Man
as did no other
Wyoming Pioneersman,
who at the last family rendezvous
bequeathed his philosophy:

My children,
the circle is about completed.
Do not try to be
too good,
do not be
too bad.
Stay in the middle
of the road and go
as far as you can.

Don't you think
it is great to push
steadily on at the task
allotted to you
and on reaching the border
to lay your burden down
and step quietly over
into that land where
trouble never enters.

WE KNOW THE RAIN FALLS

Walking our horses through the dry
grass of the greater ditch aimed toward
the great power turbines of Cheyenne,
it came on slow enough we thought
it best to leave our slickers rolled
behind the cantle; for it would
surely stop by the time
we got them.

When it began in sheets
to fall us with instant wet,
we had just stopped to pray
at the sight of a recent accident
where I dismounted to pilfer a red pair
of Dolce and Gabbana sunglasses, bedazzled
and lenses rimmed in sand. They were
beside a shattered rearview with a tassel
marked with ten draped along the ground,
still attached and willing to dangle.

We spoke few words for her,
though the girls riding with me knew
by her half empty perfume, loose
change and broken lighter
that the scene was not as settled
as the dust. Too young and too few,
the miles between us all cried
and after silent eyes and open
mouths, we joked about the lip
gloss never tasting the same,
split and gritty, about the soggy menthols
being hard to light in this cold rain.

VINCENT PAGE LYMAN

Down Breakneck Hill
once a week was enough
to tip anyone toward the old
rye, but it was none the better
over Hone Lake route
or Sander's cut-off.

Thieving habitations planted as posts
where Frenchmen and their squaws and half-
breed kids, all of size, sat.

Traded. The wigwams gathered.
Papooses lounged about one.
Spaniards lassoed a sunken post
beside the fat and standing
herd. The dust, flies. Terrible weight
yoked to the driven cattle.

WHEN THE MULE SHAVES

He is stuck between a plank
fence and an open gate,
squeezed into a scissor-ed press,
stinking and braying
through his nose—
roped off at the hinged post.

Before I was embarrassed by it,
I watched his one leg up
on the edge of the sink,
everything dangling,
nude
aside from the cream
stripped off in stripes
by the honed blade
in his hand,

and later I stretched my lower lip
into my mouth over my bottom
teeth to tighten my chin's skin
while I pretended to shave like him
in a pine tree with a piece of bark.

Running the smooth piece
about hairless cheek and top lip,
perched in low branches
like the tree was a house,
my mind watched him
shave these things, watched
my own mouth like his,
in the trunk
        of the tree,
in the crook
        of the fence and the gate.

FALLING LEAF

Named for the season
of your birth, gone
good as the badlands,
and yet to be wrinkled
but wise; on your death bed
you made your father vow
to never let arrows fly
straight and through
the pale newcomers
again.

And he was as true
as your two white
ponies tied together
to cradle your corpse
in the valley of their backs,
lashed so the hair thins
on the rubbing shoulders
and hips of your breathing,
hoof beating, good, forgiving
hearse of the great horizon.

The ground would not be dug,
your spirit instead, carried
on the wind, a stilted casket
with your head pointing east,
the tails of your ponies
on either corner post at your feet,
their heads nailed on by the ears,
an oak water bucket
beneath both stiff muzzles.

TONAWANDA, NE

You're hardly there anymore,
a few lingering foundations,
the remains of a well
covering what hole there was,
old beds stripped of fabric
to reveal the angle iron
and rusted springs.

Nothing there
that the three of us
could carry on horseback
to the asphalt a day's ride off,
nothing not covered by sand
or small enough to pocket,
all older than cherished antiques.

We rode away from our supplies
toward you, where so many
years ago, homesteaders wrapped rein
and traded for flour and sugar,
for lead and powder,
beaver and grey wolf
for whiskey and coffee.

My horse, in aluminum shoes,
snagged his right hind on a wire,
star-barbed, half-buried, and brittle
enough to be broken by hand,
and he waited, held his hoof
for me to dismount and pull
loose a catch-pen's remains

stuck between his soft frog
and the shoe loosened
by miles thought to be few
for the long-dead horses and ox
that brought us out here.

WRONG SIDE UP

Imagine watching work
when none was needed,
witnessing for the first time
longhorns stiff as blades
lined behind wagons
and trailed with dust
sweeping windward
like fingers of prairie coal
burning beneath the Dutch ovens
that hang above short grass country.

Watch, with them, the destruction
of buffalo like prairie dogs,
the way the ox and plow
pulled up the only meal
ever known to grow there,
the only roots keeping the soil
still from erosion of water
and wind while the point flips
the thin grass, roots up
for the planting of seeds
slow to grow in the sand.

MORE AND LESS, YOUR SECRET

for Meghan

"Secrets are an exalted state, almost a dream state. They're a
way of arresting motion, stopping the world so we can see
ourselves in it."
                                                    —Don DeLillo

In the mountains with 48 hooves and 11 kids,
I waited for this moment, beside Vedawoo.

Time brings season to everything,
and atop these turning wheels, dancing
in embrace, there is a place for unearthing
self in partnership where even undeserving
are catered to with love, silent
and screaming in unison.

Refraining from page and pen,
clock and calendar, it occurred
to me just as everything will be
beautiful in time, all words
find or lose meaning by the individual
soul. Spur-less, in the soft seat

of this rented car, my body far gone
from the mountains and the horses
and the kids I shared them with, the road,
moving in a constant secret dream, takes me
back to Manhattan morning and Ellerbe afternoon,
to the small spaces where we stopped

the world to see each other. The sun
in the pines rises and sets, plants and uproots,
while we spin in the deep, never-ending
starlit darkness of ever-expanding space,
and, though small, two are bigger than these
tiny spots of light, together against the night.
With 48 hooves in the mountains, family where
there was none, stones gathered around
the fire keeping cold at bay, I weep and heal
and search for the secret combination
of words to find purchase or lose it
in the eternity between merely listening

and really hearing a heart that could be
no less or no more, absolutely yours.

ACKNOWLEDGEMENTS

THERE ARE SO many people for me to thank for this collection, and most of them will never be named. There were so many saddles thrown over so many horses for so many kids at a time in their life (and mine) when everything else seemed like it needed decoding.

Ten of these poems were presented as a chapbook and three were printed as part of a Wyoming Arts Council Symposium celebrating the Arts Fellowships. Sadly, I was not able to attend due to a blizzard. I have yet to really present these poems aloud and am very excited to do so.

There are a few obvious people to thank like the Wyoming Arts Council, the University of Wyoming's staff in the archives at the Art Museum who were essential in gathering direct source material from the Pony Express station logs, and Cathedral Home for Children where I had the opportunity to cross the same rough country with the same type of kids the Pony Express targeted 150 years earlier.

Thanks to Jeff and Sally Biegert and Dick and Diane Van Pelt, who were on the board at Cathedral Home for Children and championed to make the horse program a vital part of the treatment plan for the at-risk youth served at that amazing facility just outside of Laramie, Wyoming.

My life's course was forever altered by my experiences in the mountains on horseback and in the classroom preparing to saddle up. I still wake up having dreamt of sleeping among 15 horses and kids; sloughing off a June snow dusting. There are hooves shuffling in the dark, and all of us have seen such expansive views over the day's 20 miles that we can never close our eyes again without knowing that exact freedom and possibility.

Thanks to my daughters and my lack of process around saving manuscripts, when I was almost done with this book the first time an entire mug of coffee was spilled on the computer. Lost everything but a hard copy. Thanks go out to Rachel Boice for painstakingly re-typing each and every letter. The collection is better for the destruction. My three girls have given me more joy and insight than a lifetime of reading ever could. H.L. Hix taught me that nothing in my writing is sacred. My three girls taught me that without something sacred to write about, the writer might never be able to tap into the ragged wildness of a gleefully obligated heart.

Thanks to Maggie for being a partner in my growth in all directions of my life. I am a man of many costumes, and Maggie's been beside me at each stop. She's always quick to ask me what I'm writing; to be so loved. Thanks to her, I know how to block my calendar so I can write and still get my job(s) done.

Thanks to my great friend and poet, Ben Gotschall! He read and reread these poems in much worse condition than they find you today.

My parents, Mike and Sue Renken, have asked me at least a dozen times when my next book would be out. They have pushed me to create space for myself and art my entire life; taught me to beg forgiveness before asking permission.

There's a whole slew of colleagues to thank in Atlanta and Charlotte too. I work with a group of uncompromising professionals who have pushed me to put every moment of my time to its highest and best use. Thankfully, that's given me the time and space to sing my song.

ABOUT THE AUTHOR

SAMUEL STENGER RENKEN received his BA at Nebraska Wesleyan with the late great Bill Kloefkorn, an MA at Clemson with Keith Lee Morris, and an MFA in Wyoming with H.L. Hix. This is his second collection of poetry. He is currently Managing Director of Consolidated Planning Atlanta.